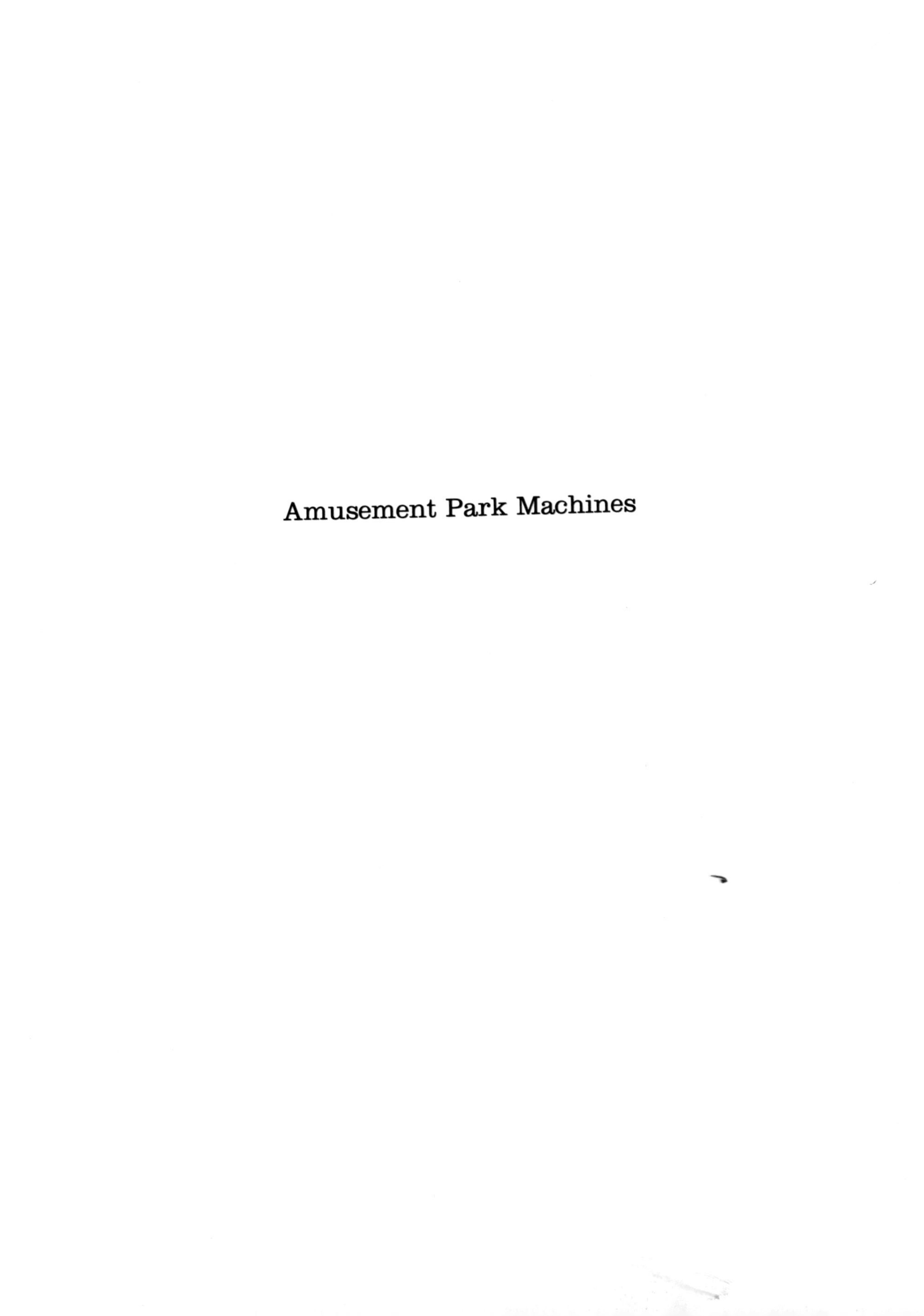

Amusement Park Machines

Inquiries should be addressed to Raintree Childrens Books, 205 West Highland Avenue, Milwaukee, Wisconsin 53203.

Library of Congress Number: 78-26920

3 4 5 6 7 8 9 0 83 82 81 80

Printed in the United States of America.

Library of Congress Cataloging in Publication Data

Hahn, Christine.
Amusement park machines.

Includes index.
SUMMARY: Describes the various kinds of machines, primarily those for rides, found in amusement parks and what they do.
1. Amusement rides — Juvenile literature.
[1. Amusement rides] I. Title.
GV1859.H33 688.7 78-26920
ISBN 0-8172-1330-9 lib. bdg.

Cover illustration: Jerry Scott

Photographs appear through the courtesy of the following companies:

Atari: p. 29
Cedar Point, photographs by Daniel L. Feicht: pp. 3, 5 (top), 6 (bottom), 7, 16, 17, 18, 26, 30
Chance Manufacturing Company: p. 13
Hersheypark: p. 6 (top)
King's Island: pp. 10 (top), 14, 22 (bottom), 23
Magic Mountain: pp. 20, 21, 22 (top), 27
Marriott's Great America: pp. 4, 5 (bottom), 9 (bottom), 10 (bottom), 12
Opryland: pp, 8, 24, 25, 28
Sellner Manufacturing Company: p. 11
Six Flags over Texas: pp. 9 (top), 15

amusement park MACHINES

Christine Hahn

RAINTREE CHILDRENS BOOKS
Milwaukee • Toronto • Melbourne • London

Most machines are built for work. But some machines are built just for fun. You find these "fun" machines in fairgrounds, carnivals, and amusement parks all over the world.

Did you ever look at the machines at an amusement park? Some are simple. Some are not. Some go fast and high. Some swing you around and around. Some make you scream.

The merry-go-round was one of the first amusement park rides. You sit on brightly colored animals and go round and round. Sometimes you move up and down at the same time.

Some merry-go-rounds have thousands of colored lights. Many play music as you ride.

There are many other rides that go in circles. Some of them swing you at the end of a steel arm. Most of these rides are near the ground. But some swing you round very high up.

Some rides turn in circles inside other circles. While the whole machine turns in one circle, your seat turns around in another circle.

These big machines are usually called Ferris wheels. They carry you high above the amusement park. Some Ferris wheels turn in circles inside other circles.

This machine spins around at great speed. Your back is pushed hard against the outside screen. Then the floor drops away. But you don't fall down.

These cars go round the top of the loop so fast that you cannot fall out.

You don't fall out of these rides, either. That is because the train takes you up very fast. When the train turns upside down, you still push up so hard that you stay in your seat. And the train pushes up so hard that it stays on the track.

Many loop rides are part of a bigger ride—the biggest ride of all. It is called a roller coaster. Thousands of feet of track take you up and down and around. You may speed as fast as 60 miles an hour.

Some roller coasters take you high in the air.

Others don't go high at all.

Many amusement parks have water rides. You sit in a boat and float down a long slide. Then you splash into the water.

SIX FLAGS

The parachute ride is one of the highest of all. You sit in a seat and go slowly up and up. When you reach the top, down you come — floating through the air.

On this ride, you sit in a cab that moves slowly along a strong cable. You can see the whole amusement park.

Some amusement parks have a high tower. You ride up in an elevator. From the top, you look down on all the rides.

Another way to see the park is by taking a ride on the train.

Not all the fun is on the rides. There are also pinball machines. The metal balls race around the board — off the bumpers and through the gates. Lights flash. Buzzers buzz. Bells ring.

GLOSSARY

amusement park	An area with many rides, games, shows, and places to eat. Amusement parks stay in one place for long periods of time.
cable ride	A ride in a car that hangs from a long, strong cable. The rides are high above the ground.
carnival	An area like an amusement park, but smaller. Carnivals are usually set up for a few days.
fairground	Any place where rides, games, shows, and games are set up.
Ferris wheel	A big wheel with seats around the rim. As the wheel turns, you ride round to the top and back down again.
loop ride	A fast ride on a track that turns upside down in circles and loops.
merry-go-round	An old-fashioned ride that takes you round and round and up and down, on painted animals.
parachute	A huge sheet of cloth that floats you gently to the ground. It is shaped like an umbrella. It holds you underneath in a seat fixed to ropes.
pinball machine	A machine with a metal ball that goes into a maze that has flashing lights, buzzers, and bells. The longer you keep the ball moving, the more points you score.
roller coaster	A fast ride that takes you up and down and around on thousands of feet of track.

INDEX